The White Rose

Defending Freedom

Veronica Finch

The White Rose UK

The White Rose

Defending Freedom

Veronica Finch

The White Rose UK

Contents

	Preface	8
1	A Gentle Resistance	11
2	About the White Rose UK (as published on the website)	16
3	Poem—A White Rose	21
4	It's Evil	23
5	Emails	25
6	How Did We Get This Far?	35
7	Other White Rose Groups	42
8	Poem—Don't Be Silenced	44
9	Protests	46
10	It's All the Opposite of What They Say	50
11	Depopulation	52
12	Leafleting	55
13	The White Rose UK Leaflets	58

14 English Translations of the German White Rose Leaflets   77

15 Appendix: Resources   102

Dedication

Dedicated to all warriors of the truth.

Preface

Some people reproach us for using the same organisation name as the heroes of World War II. They say we should be ashamed and things like that. These people do not realise that, in the early 1940s, those young heroes were treated in a similar fashion. While carrying out their brave actions within the resistance, they were not cheered as heroes, nor did they enjoy acknowledgement.

In their days, it was a disgrace to say anything against the regime. In the end, it was the 'politically correct' people who snitched on them, leading to their deaths. One of my family members also brought to my attention that, in the days of the Bible, prophets were first despised and then killed before being celebrated as heroes, all by the same kind of people.

Thankfully, many others understand that what we are doing is not a misuse of the name White Rose. They understand that comparing these days with the Nazi regime is not an overstatement. They recognise in our governments the same misuse of power, the pattern of lies and deceit, and the suppression of freedom, and they are aware, that the true horrors will only reveal themselves, when it is already too late.

Some compare these days to the 1930s in Germany, when hardly anyone was aware of what atrocities were developing in the background but the signs, such as the discrimination of the Jews in public, were already apparent. Where is the difference today? We are on the verge of becoming an apartheid of the vaccinated and unvaccinated; where the unvaccinated will not have access to various public places, to jobs and education, just like the Jews were denied in Nazi Germany.

The Nazi regime's reach was felt mostly in Germany and several other European countries. What is happening now is effecting the whole globe.

Would those who accuse us of misusing the name White Rose still think the same, if they knew that hundreds of thousands of elderly care home residents were murdered during this alleged pandemic? That, in the UK, millions were denied treatment, which resulted in tens of thousands of unnecessary excess deaths? That over a million adverse reactions and over 1,700 deaths from the covid jab have been reported, and that may only be 1–10% of all cases? What would they say if they knew that millions more are going to die due to the experimental jab? It is not even a vaccine but a type of gene therapy, and it is being used intentionally to reduce the population.

In other words, it is causing a global genocide.

We hardly ever hear a word in the media about the famines in Africa and Asia caused by the lockdowns. We also don't know yet to what extent the health of millions of people around the world will be effected by hours of daily mask wearing and by test swabs which can cause damage to the pineal gland and could possibly vaccinate people without their knowing. Add to this the surge of mental health problems and suicides, and it is not hard to picture that lockdowns, covid restrictions and covid injections are and will be the cause of billions of deaths worldwide—unless people stop complying to the madness today.

Fortunately, there are many people who are committed to the truth and would rather endure harassment than act against their conscience.

If the majority acted in this way, the global dictatorship would not be able to gain a foothold in the world, and those in power would not be able to carry out their evil plan against humanity.

Veronica Finch, November 2021

1

A Gentle Resistance

The only thing we need to be afraid of coming from China, is communism, not the virus.
(A comment I made in January 2020)

What inspired me to begin with the White Rose UK was the German underground resistance group, called Die weisse Rose, which fought against the Nazis in the 1940's. Their movement gives us an example of peaceful resistance in dark times. Like the attributes of a white rose, Die weisse Rose was a gentle resistance, powered by hope in what is good. This hope has survived for decades and is still alive today. Even though the young siblings, Sophie and Hans Scholl, and other members of Die Weisse Rose were brutally executed by means of the guillotine, their legacy is alive. A friend of the Scholls expressed it with these words: '... their spirit lives on'.

From my diary:
I watched the film 'Die weisse Rose' (The White Rose) again. It's about a German underground resistance movement during World War II. I have already watched this film, many years ago, and I am equally inspired by the initiative of these brave young Germans. After the film I read all six flyers that the members of the White Rose wrote and distributed. I found amazing parallels to what is going on right now, and I feel inspired to write something similar myself. Maybe a kind of continuation of the White Rose?
(28/5/2020)

The first time I heard about Sophie Scholl, I was a teenager. I was touched by the film Die weisse Rose (produced 1982), and when I watched almost three decades later I was equally impressed and encouraged to find out more about them.

Today we are once again confronted with a dangerous power grab. This time the intention is to control the entire world. Truth is being censored while we are showered with untruths from the government. A silent genocide is happening in the background, without a single gunshot, but with the consent of all the brainwashed. Crowds of people are masked and muzzled, while lining up for a dangerous and deadly 'vaccine'. The so-called vaccine was in the plan from the beginning of this orchestrated pandemic.

But there is hope. We, the people, outweigh the small globalist rulership, and if the majority finally wake up from their dangerous lethargy, the evil elite, who is leading this terrible agenda, will have to succumb. I don't know when that day will be; all I know is that that day will come. Just as the Nazi terror had to come to an end, albeit with a lot of victims, this covid fraud will also end. And then a new era will arise—because when the great lie falls, many other lies will fall with it—all the lies and deceits this government, the mainstream media and those behind them have pushed upon us for years. The whole construct will crumble, it's just a matter of time.

But for now, we are in the middle of the biggest fraud history has ever seen.

The White Rose UK began with a long flyer that I wrote with the intention to distribute it. It was completed on Whitsunday 2020. On that same day, I discovered a white peony blossoming in our garden, even though, in previous years, the peonies growing on the same bush were pink. Peony is named Pfingstrose in German, which translates into Whitsunday rose. It's hard to imagine that this was just a coincidence. But the leaflet remained undistributed for some time.

> From my diary:
> *I've finished a draft called The Continuation of the White Rose. It is a three-page letter dated on Pentecost, aka Whitsunday. When I went through our back garden this morning, I discovered white peonies blossoming! Neither my husband nor I remember seeing white ones before. In previous years the same peonies grew in pink. These white peonies were also blossoming exactly on Pentecost. In German they are called Pfingstrosen, which would mean Pentecost roses. Since I've been thinking a lot about the White Rose recently and writing The Continuation, the blossoming of these peonies are like a supernatural symbol.*
>
> (31 May 2020)

Shortly before taking part in a large protest, in late summer 2020, I rewrote the flyer and printed several of them for handing out on the streets of London. After that I rewrote it again, and when the website was up and running in November 2020, and I had published a request for proofreaders, we got plenty of offers. One of those offering their help looked through the leaflet and did some editing. The result from his editing was a well written leaflet we then began distributing in the hundreds and hundreds, and also kept updating as things evolved.

Two of my older children and my husband joined in with leafleting. We added it on the website for people to download and distribute themselves. To people who weren't able to print, we sent off packages with dozens or hundreds of leaflets. We handed out leaflets on the streets, brought them to people's homes through the door, stuck them in car door handles and under windscreen wipers, left them in shops, at cash machines and in churches.

When we went online in November, and during the time I was still commenting on the Daily Telegraph website, where there was a surprisingly great amount of lockdown sceptics (I got blocked twice for spreading information against the covid 'vaccine'), we soon had a handful of subscribers to our weekly newsletter. The number of subscribers quickly increased, especially around January 2021, when someone with a lot of followers published a link to our website. At that time we gained dozens of new subscribers on a daily basis. There is now a growing list of around 5,500 subscribers. Our weekly newsletter contains up to 28 posts from the news section, the result of hours of research done by myself or by our readers. In March 2021 we published a book entitled *Freedom!* It contains poems, short stories and essays from 36 authors questioning covid restrictions and lockdowns.

The bedrock of the White Rose lies in Christian faith, just as it did for the German Weisse Rose. Christian faith, when understood properly, provides us with the foundation for peaceful, non-violent resistance. Christ's message was always a message of authentic love, gentleness and peace—even when he said 'I have not come to bring peace (on earth), but a sword.' His 'sword' is the sword of truth. Whoever doesn't choose truth will submit to division. A lot of evil in the world is due to people hiding from the truth and following lies.

The members of die Weisse Rose were able to clearly distinguish between good and evil. Maybe one of the main problems of our time is that we cannot distinguish so well between good and bad. That way we have become easily manipulative and brainwashed. If we hold on to Christian faith, we are always on the side of the truth, because Jesus Christ Himself is the Truth.

Truth is powerful, beautiful and pure, but also gentle and vulnerable—like a white rose. Getting to the truth can sometimes be painful—just like the thorns of a rose when they prick you. Yet the sweet smell of the rose is pleasant. In its gentleness, a white rose also symbolises humility. Humility is the path to truth. Only by being humble we are able to get through to the truth. Humility is the path to heaven.

We don't need to do great things to be influential. We can do small things and still make a great difference. To demonstrate how the Kingdom of God can spread by doing little things, without having the advantage of being well-known or popular, Jesus used the parable of the woman who makes sourdough bread. While preparing the dough, she adds a little sourdough, which eventually turns the whole dough sour which results in wonderful bread. We too can be that sourdough. By distributing leaflets and spreading the truth we are contributing to the wake-up call of society.

We can only shape our present and future together with God. Without including God, we will achieve nothing but destruction, division and hate. With God we will achieve peace and freedom.

2

About the White Rose UK
(as published on the website)

The White Rose UK is a peaceful resistance group based in the UK. It all began shortly before Whitsunday in the year 2020, when it became apparent that covid-19 was no more dangerous than the flu and that covid restrictions, imposed by our government, were clearly violating our basic human rights.

On our website we publish articles, videos and other information that help people to become more aware of what is going on. We also offer leaflets for distribution. Please share our news and leaflets widely. Let us all unite to fight the good fight.

The truth will make you free (John 8:32)

Mask mandatory? Social distancing? Lockdown after lockdown? Loneliness and depression? Forced vaccination? Ruined businesses and livelihoods? Silent genocide through depopulation? We say NO! We have recognised that the covid restrictions are destructive and deeply dehumanising. A virus that is less dangerous than the flu, is being used as an excuse to turn the world into a new kind of global communism. For the sake of our children, and their children, we peacefully resist this evil evolvement. We say NO! to new normal because it is entirely abnormal and inhumane.

The truth will set you free! Read, download and print out our leaflets. Share them among friends, family, neighbours and strangers. Visit our website and subscribe to our newsletter to stay updated on upcoming events.

Join the peaceful movement to restore our freedom, our rights and our humanity.

ORIGIN OF THE WHITE ROSE

'We will not keep silent, we are your guilty conscience;
the White Rose will not leave you in peace!'
                    (Die Weisse Rose)

During World War II a German underground movement called Die Weisse Rose (The White Rose) distributed leaflets calling on people to resist the Nazi regime. One of their leaflets mentioned that every single human is entitled to a government that guarantees the freedom of every single person and the wellbeing of the community. Every human should be able to reach their natural goal, their earthly joy, autonomously and by their own accord. Die Weisse Rose spoke to people's conscience and urged them to wake up from their dangerous lethargy. In their fourth leaflet the members of Die Weisse Rose wrote: 'We will not keep silent, we are your guilty conscience; the White Rose will not leave you in peace!'

The German resistance group consisted of the students Sophie Scholl and her brother Hans Scholl, as well as their friend Christoph Probst and single other members. Coming from a Christian background, the Scholl siblings turned back to Christian morality after having spent some time in the Hitler Youth. Spreading anti-regime leaflets was a dangerous activity, and after being caught, several members of the Weisse Rose were sentenced to death or imprisonment by the Nazis. After the executions of the siblings Scholl, a friend still carried on with distributing leaflets entitled 'And their spirit lives on.' With this in mind, the White Rose UK is part of the continuation.

The disproportionate and dehumanising covid restrictions are a disgrace to humanity. Masks, social distancing and the so-called vaccination are causing great harm. People protesting against lockdowns have been arrested and treated like criminals for gathering and exercising their right of free speech. At the same time, YouTube, Facebook and Twitter have been censoring videos and posts that do not match the current trend of the mainstream media. Schools have now turned into social engineering sites. Forcing children to wear masks and keeping children constantly at a distance in class and on school grounds is deeply dehumanising, and will have a damaging effect on children's mental development. Parents should stand up against these guinea-pig methods. It's not the way we grew up, and we should make sure our children grow up with the same freedoms we enjoyed!

Many experts have warned that the so-called covid vaccines will do a lot of harm, and now with over a million adverse reactions—many of them severe—and over one thousand seven hundred reported deaths in the UK alone, there is proof that the covid jab is causing great harm.

Bit by bit, we have given up our freedom and our rights out of fear of a virus. After the first lockdown it was evident that more people died from the lockdown than from the virus. Our economy will suffer severely and poverty will increase. How many people have lost their job and how many businesses are ruined due to the lockdowns?

The so-called 'new normal' is not normal, it's entirely abnormal and we should never get used to it! It's time to take over responsibility and to make decisions for ourselves, or else, the next generation of grown-ups will not experience the same freedom we've had before this manufactured covid crisis.

Like the White Rose in Germany, that resisted the Nazi regime, we encourage people to resist the covid tyranny. We do not want any more lockdowns and demand an end to all restrictions. Visit your friends and family, the lonely, the vulnerable and the dying. We are humans and not controllable robots. We need to socially interact, without anti-social distancing and without face masks.

Journalists, teachers, doctors, lawyers, politicians should stand up for the truth and speak out publicly. If the majority of people rid themselves of fear and panic and make use of common sense, those who want to control us will eventually have to give up, and we will be able to guarantee a future of peace and freedom for our children and grandchildren.

With continuing the White Rose in the UK we are driven by the same spirit as the German Weisse Rose during Nazi Germany—a spirit that comes from the conscience and rises against injustice; a spirit nurtured by the depth of the heart where truth is embedded.

SYMBOLISM OF THE WHITE ROSE

A white rose stands for peace, purity and innocence. In religious tradition, a white rose symbolises the purity of the Mother of Christ.

We believe that humanity was created out of love and for a good reason. Therefore, it is our duty to defend the dignity of every human! Peace and love originate in God, who is the creator of the world. Without truth and without love there can be no peace—without peace, there can be no freedom. Pray with us that His Kingdom may come!

THE WHITE ROSE
AND THE CATHOLIC CHRISTIAN FAITH

The White Rose UK has been founded by lay Catholics and is supported by Christians of all denominations, as well as people of other faiths and none.

The Scholls and other members of the original White Rose in Germany, were inspired by the sermons of Catholic Bishop Von Galen and the writings of John Henry Newman (a former Anglican who converted into the Catholic Church and has recently been canonized). The pamphlets they wrote were influenced by these theologians who belonged to a network of Catholic priests and altar servers who initially spread leaflets with anti-Nazi homilies. Christoph Probst, another member of The White Rose, grew up without religion, but requested baptism and was received in the Catholic Church shortly before his execution. The Scholls themselves were drawn to the Catholic Church.

3

Poem—A White Rose

I saw a white rose, sweet and delicate
Only gentle wind touched and moved it
But when the sun set at the horizon
Dark clouds overlay my chosen one.

The sun was gone and with it all light
Darkness surrounded the rose so white
Thunder rumbled, lightnings flashed
A loud bang, as dark clouds clashed.

The white rose, pure and soft
Was torn and pushed around a lot
The wind tore and tugged the blossom
It lost its petals, all but one.

The wind shook it like a rattle
Heavy rain tore down the last petal
A stormy wind snapped off its head
The white rose now appeared to be dead.

Next morning petals lay on the ground
Covering the grave all around
Nothing was left apart from branch and scent
The rose bush entered its secret Lent.

Autumn passed and winter froze
Snow-covered memories of my white rose
Nothing was left of the blossom at all
Nothing but white rose's faint call.

Then spring came, and like a joyful wife
The white rose's twig sprang back to life
First a green bud, that then turned white
Who would've thought it'd win the fight?

From the desolate branch with no flower head
A new rose flower arose from the dead
Not only one, but three and four
And glancing around, I discovered more.

4

It's Evil

It's evil to keep us apart, preventing us from seeing each other or staying meters apart. No closeness, no hug, no sense of the other.

It's evil to keep our faces covered, and all we see are anxious eyes. We don't see a smile or any other facial expression.

It's evil to tell us where to stand or where not to, which side to walk and which spot to wait on—just to keep us apart.

It's evil to 'act as if you've got it' (governmental propaganda). Aren't they telling us to lie?

'Hands, face, space!' they chant into our unconsciousness along with the daily death counts and case counts, which are laughable if it weren't so evil. I don't watch TV and seldom read the mainstream news. I rather watch documentaries and commentaries with more insight and proper reporting, than biased media not telling the truth.

It is evil to bombard us with their constant propaganda that makes people fearful, expecting their neighbour to be a constant threat to their health.

It is evil what they're doing to the children—forcing them to wear masks that are bad for their physical and psychological health.

It's evil the way they've locked down the country several times, closing small businesses for ever, causing depressions and despair.

It's evil that patients who needed hospital treatment were turned away while hospital departments were empty. It's evil how untreated and undiagnosed illnesses are leading to much higher death rates than those of the virus.

It's evil how they're coercing us all to get a covid 'vaccination', although covid is hardly a threat to anyone. It's evil how the 'vaccine' is killing people and will kill many more, and they aren't talking about it.

It's evil to mention that a few hundred were demonstrating in London, although there were a hundred thousand. It's evil how they usually don't mention peaceful protest marches, and if they do, then only from a negative perspective.

There's much more I could list here. The whole event is a clever, genius plan. But it's evil, evil, evil!

5

Emails

We receive dozens of emails everyday. Some people just want to express their heartfelt gratitude for the work we do and send their blessings. Some come up with questions and suggestions for publishing on the website, ask for an interview, or just pour out their heart over the terrible crimes that are happening. People write to say they are worried about their loved-ones who have had or are about to have the covid shot. Under the 'Things to Do' category on the website, are possible remedies for detoxing the destructive spike protein (found in the covid injection) and vaccine shedding, (which could harm people who have chosen not to be injected).

We also get abusive emails from people, which I usually ignore. I wonder if they will once regret their insults and curses, once this is all over?

Sometimes I make an exception and answer a negative email, for example when the person's statements are typical for those who still believe in the covid fraud, or if someone seems to be asking honest questions. Here is such an answer:

> *Dear...*
> *I think you are wrong in several ways. It is easy to humiliate others and call everything a conspiracy theory when you haven't done your own or not enough research. In other words, you are judging out of laziness or simply out of fear because you don't want to face the facts.*
> *It is the government that has been spreading misinformation and brainwashing people into believing that*

the virus is the deadliest illness humanity has ever experienced. And it's not a coincidence. They are part of an evil global conspiracy that has the intention to enslave humanity and enforce transhumanism. It's all part of the so-called Great Reset, aka Agenda 21.

If you have seen people suffering from the virus, then ask yourself if you have never seen people suffering from illnesses before. We've never shut down the entire country, introduced mass vaccination or vaccine passes because of the flu or any other illness with far greater fatality rates. This virus is not deadlier than the flu. Do your research and take a look at history (Nazis, communism, etc.). Some people are capable of a lot of evil.

If you want to think about the wellbeing of others, stop the virtue signalling and wake up before it's too late.

Kind regards

Among the more vicious emails there was once someone claiming that he had caused our online shop to be taken down. We had signed up to an online shop before, which enabled us to offer a few products (hoodies, t-shirts etc.) with the logo and slogan from the White Rose UK, and earn a small percentage from each sale. The shop was taken down because the White Rose UK was allegedly opposed to their guidelines. I wrote an email to the business explaining to them, why I thought they were wrong. The same individual who admitted being responsible for reporting us, also said he'd do the same to our PayPal account where people are able to donate. Luckily, our PayPal account has remained untouched till today. When we tried a second time to have an online shop, it got cancelled again. Eventually, we decided to order bulk and ship the t-shirt orders ourselves.

This is what I wrote to Teespring, in response to them deleting our online sales due to the 'spread of misinformation':

There is no misinformation on our website. Please do your own research. We have published experts from all around the world warning about the content of the so-called covid vaccine.

Why do you trust the Pharma industry more than doctors, professors, virologists who are experts on the subject and are not profiting from warning everyone, whilst the Pharma industry is getting billions out of the 'vaccine' propaganda? Why do you believe their lies? Do you know that we are now experiencing a silent unprecedented genocide?

What you are really doing by forbidding us to sell t-shirts is suppressing free speech. I would like to know on what basis you have made the decision. Has someone with ill intent reported our site? Why do you listen to them instead of carrying out your own investigation?

Unfortunately, if you remain with your decision I will let people know that your business is suppressing free speech and is also supporting propaganda for a highly dangerous drug. There are already over 822,000 averse side effects and over 1,200 deaths reported in the UK alone—and that is just a small percentage of all cases, because not every case gets reported.

Please do your own research, this is serious. Humanity is under the greatest threat ever.

Kind regards

Just like Facebook, Twitter and YouTube, both online shops, Spreadshirt and Teespring, are following the current narrative, and censoring anything that goes against it. These days you can get banned for telling the truth, for spreading scientific facts and for speaking up against the fraud. There are enough other options to choose from, so people are swarming to platforms like Telegram, Brandnewtube, Bitchute, Rumble and Odysee, where free speech is allowed.

Here are more answers to emails received. The following two emails are responses to individuals who had some reservations towards the White Rose's connection to faith:

Dear...
Thank you for contacting the White Rose and for your honest questions. I will try my best to answer them, although this is not a simple task.
You mention the 'absence of any evidence of a higher being ...' Here I may note that for many people who believe in God, there is more evidence of His existence rather than of His non-existence. For example, if you look at the fact that for us, life is only possible on planet earth, and if you look at all the hidden and obvious rules of nature and how everything is made—you may discover that this is all not a coincidence but made according to a genius plan. Science and religion do not contradict, and there are great scientists who believe in the existence of God.
So, if you know that there is a higher being, or indeed God The Creator behind all of this, then you also will find it easier to understand, that God became a human in order to show solidarity with the human race. God was born as Jesus Christ (the Saviour), who was fully human and fully God. He suffered as a human, felt and lived as a human, his only difference to us humans was that he remained without sin.
This indeed again is not a 2000 year old conspiracy, it is an invitation to believe in our reason for existing, and an invitation to believe in God's love towards you and me. Jesus Christ was a real person—even the Romans, who were then non-Christian, have recorded the historical figure of a man crucified called Jesus Christ. Furthermore, it is exactly in the Bible where you will

find warnings of times like these. If you read the Revelation (last part of the New Testament) you will find a place where John mentions that there will be a time where people will get the mark of the beast, and only those with it will be able to buy and trade etc. Many believe that the 'vaccine' is the mark of the beast (satanic) and interestingly, the patent number for the Microsoft cryptocurrency system using body activity contains the 666. For these and other reasons, it is no coincidence why Christians (and people of other faiths) do not find it hard to expose the covid fraud.

Hope this helps ...

Kind regards,

This is the place where the mark of the beast is mentioned in the Bible:

From the Book of Revelation, Chapter 13 (Revised Standard Version Catholic Edition):

The Second Beast

'Then I saw another beast which rose out of the earth; it had two horns like a lamb and it spoke like a dragon. It exercises all the authority of the first beast in its presence, and makes the earth and its inhabitants worship the first beast, whose mortal wound was healed. It works great signs, even making fire come down from heaven to earth in the sight of men; and by the signs which it is allowed to work in the presence of the beast, it deceives those who dwell on earth, bidding them make an image for the beast which was wounded by the sword and yet lived; and it was allowed to give breath to the image of the beast so that the image of the beast should even speak, and to cause those who would not worship the image of the beast to be slain. Also it causes all, both small and great, both rich and poor, both free and slave, to be marked on the right hand or the forehead, so that no one can buy or sell unless he has the mark, that is, the name of the beast or the number of its name. This calls for wisdom: let him who has understanding reckon the number of the beast, for it is a human number, its number is six hundred and six-ty-six.'

> *Hi...*
> *Thank you for contacting the White Rose UK!*
> *As you may guess, I can't fully agree with you. You may be right that with 'leaving God out of it' might be more appealing to certain people, but it wouldn't be the right thing to do. Firstly, I believe we can't improve the whole situation without God (who is the source of true love, peace and freedom), and secondly, the original White Rose that began in Germany, was founded by a group of people who were Christians. It was exactly their Christian faith that inspired them to do something against the Nazi terror and to prevent evil from spreading.*
> *Best wishes,*

Some answers to a person, who was trying to find some sense in all of this:

> *Hi...*
> *Thanks for contacting the White Rose UK and for showing your interest. I will try to answer some of your questions.*
> *For the great majority of us covid is no threat at all, not more than the flu. If you aren't very vulnerable, I don't believe there is a reason to be afraid. The fear comes from all the propaganda which has been imposed on us for over a year. I highly recommend you listen to videos with Dr Sucharit Bhakdi or read his book—Corona, False Alarm. There is a recent video with Bhakdi under 'News' on our website.*

I do agree that some theories don't hold water. But a lot of what some people still call conspiracy theories, aren't theories anymore, they are just facts. For example, the plan of the Great Reset and Agenda 21, or the vax pass were all once supposed to be conspiracy theories, but are now no secret anymore. Everyone can look up and find out that there is a plan, and what is happening now is not coincidence.

The 'gain' for government and big business is that they will become even more powerful and wealthy. From a spiritual prospective, of course, nothing of that is a true gain. It is just their evil and greed taking overhand. The core of it is satanism. Keeping us at home is part of an evil plan to destroy humanity, rather than to protect us for health reasons. You may be aware that more deaths result from lockdowns than from the virus. Masks are also harmful and utterly useless in regards to viruses.

The White Rose has nothing to do with supremacist, rightist symbolism. Maybe people have become a bit colour crazed, these days? Check out about the origins of the White Rose here: https://thewhiterose.uk/about.

Our White Rose group is also not linked to any anarchist groups.

There has always been the flu and other illnesses around, but it seems people have forgotten that, and all they see is covid, covid, covid.

The plan behind this is more than Hancock et al wanting to 'line their pockets'. As mentioned above, it's all about Agenda 21 and a New World Order. In other words, they want a communist style global regime along with depopulation and transhumanism. You'll find more interesting resources on our website ... keep on digging!

Hope that helps!

Best wishes,

Sometimes people also ask for help in search of an English lawyer to defend them against being pressurised to having to take the covid 'vaccine', or when they want to know how they can defend themselves from having to wear a mask or being forced to take a PCR test. Although I'm not an expert in legal matters, I try to help.

In one email a man wrote on behalf of his friend who received a £200 fine for not wearing a mask on a bus in London.

> *Hi...*
> *Sorry to hear about your friend's trouble. Nobody can be forced to wear a mask—it is simply against our human rights. If he's 'exempt' then he shouldn't even have to show an exemption card—that is according to the government rules. On the government's own website you can also read that you don't need to wear a mask if it causes harm to you or others. Now, to be precise, the mask does cause harm to oneself and others, especially in the long term. So, basically he could argue with that in mind.*
> *See here under 'When you do not need to wear a face covering': https://www.gov.uk/government/publications/face-coverings-when-to-wear-one-and-how-to-make-your-own/face-coverings-when-to-wear-one-and-how-to-make-your-own*
> *Prof Dolores Cahill about travelling in freedom: https://thewhiterose.uk/covid-travel-prison/*
> *Hope that helps a little.*
>
> *It is a real disgrace that people are being assaulted and punished for not wearing a mask that is useless and harmful.*
> *He could argue that wearing a mask causes distress— which would be a reason for not having to wear one.*

On the government's website it says you don't have to wear one... 'where putting on, wearing or removing a face covering will cause you severe distress'.

We have some articles about the masks on the website which show how bad mask wearing is—for his defence. See here (keyword in the search: 'mask') https://the-whiterose.uk/?s=mask

Best wishes

A man wrote to us complaining about adverse reactions after receiving the covid jab:

This is just a quick testimony (and I'm sure that you've heard this many times) about my recent experience with the so-called 'vaccine'.

After a year of fairly good health, I received my summons to go and have the jab. I had to go as I'm waiting for a life changing operation, and it was made very clear to me that unless I do this, the operation will never happen.

Since then (surprise, surprise), I have experienced nothing but endless health issues. I cannot climb stairs, my sense of taste and smell are effected (I constantly smell urine wherever I go), I'm in constant pain, and I've suffered from acute insomnia. Thankfully, the symptoms are beginning to ease after four long weeks.

Will I go to seek medical advice on this? Like Hell I will! Will I go for my second jab? Like Hell I will, and damn the consequences! Our bodies are designed to let us know when something is wrong, and this was the mother of all wake up calls! Rest assured that as soon as I feel well enough I will be giving you every means of support and assistance that I can.

From the many grateful emails, here two examples:

I want to sincerely thank you for all your tremendous work and information. You have helped me beyond measure. I love truth and I believe lies originate with Satan. Your work has affected me greatly.

Just a very short message to you all. These are dark times indeed, but you create light and hope with your brilliant website. Thank you, for everything!

Emails not only reach us from England, requests and comments also come from Wales, Scotland, from overseas such as France, Spain and as far as Australia, USA and Canada. After the huge freedom march on 24 April, I even received emails from America asking for advice as to how they could organise a march there.

It's always good to know there are like-minded people all over the world, who share the same values and are striving for the truth.

6

How Did We Get This Far?

NO PROBLEM?

When a delivery woman once came to fetch a packet from home, I intended to hand it over into her hands. This would be the natural thing to do. But, while she stood a few metres away from me, I was told to put the packet on the floor, so that she could pick it up from there and after that she'd pop the receipt through my door.

'No problem,' I answered politely. Then I asked myself: Is there really no problem in this behaviour? Well, actually, there is a problem. It's a massive problem! People have been trained to approach each other as if they were enemies; we have been trained to behave like robots, while our human contact has been minimized. That is a great problem.

SHOULD WE PRAY FOR PEOPLE LIKE BILL GATES AND KLAUS SCHWAB?

Yes, I think we should. Their influence on businesses, institutions and the media are immense. They are the wealthy and powerful, the ones who rule with money. They are deeply immersed in a darkness that is reaching every part of the earth, like a virus spreading all over the world. We should pray for their conversion. Yes, we should feel deeply sorry for their souls. They are at the root of a lot of malady and have caused a lot of evil. God save their souls. Their conversion could cause a lot of change.

WHAT IF THE INTERNET IS GONE TOMORROW?

They have made us very much dependant on the internet; so much has gone online. We should write diaries and publish books so that we can keep physical testimonies of these times. One day they will be found in an attic, in a cellar or stored away in a wardrobe. And in case history gets rewritten by those who are now at power, those written testimonies will speak the full truth.

THEY'VE PLANNED A LOT, BUT THEY HAVEN'T RECKONED WITH GOD

The self-elected elite are trying to dictate to everyone how to live, and they want to vaccinate the world with a false vaccine in order, to achieve their depopulation plan. They are the makers of Agenda 21 and The Great Reset which they intend to deploy in order to manipulate the world to their agenda. Their plan is going ahead, and they're quite successful in it. They have brainwashed hundreds of millions into believing the fraud.

But they haven't reckoned with one thing. And that is God. They haven't reckoned with God. Whenever he decides it to be the right time, he will overturn their plan. One day the whole setup of lies will collapse like a house of cards. It's only a matter of time.

VACCINE ADVERSE REACTIONS AND POINTLESS PCR TESTS

A friend's mum who had some pre-conditions (arthritis, mobility problems and mild asthma) was pressurised into having the covid injection. Immediately after receiving the jab, she had to be admitted to hospital, due to a sudden swelling of the body. From then on she was paralysed neck downwards, and was cared for at her daughter's home. A few months later, she died as a result of these adverse reactions to the covid jab.

At the end of June, the Yellow Card report system (you can find it on UK Column News) showed around a million adverse reactions and over 1,400 deaths after the covid injections. It is estimated that only 1–10% of all adverse reactions are being reported.

The daughter of this same friend, who attends a reputable boarding school, had to undergo a 24-hour lockdown. The reason for this was the fact that a schoolmate produced a positive PCR test result. A whole group of youngsters was then ordered to remain in their bedrooms for the next 24 hours. This is extraordinary and could be called torture. If anyone should ever be quarantined, it would be the sick person if they'd be a potential danger to others. But we all know by now that children and young adults have practically zero chance of dying from covid. Above that, the PCR has been proved to produce over 90% false positives (according to the inventor, the test was never made for this purpose)—and according to Dr Mike Yeadon (former VP of Pfizer) you cannot pass on covid when asymptomatic, when you don't have the illness and don't show any symptoms.

SHOPPING

From the day masks became mandatory, I hadn't been to any supermarket for almost nine months (apart from one or the other smalls shops). But because I wanted to get clothes for an upcoming child's birthday, I decided to put up with it and go to Morrison's, despite their radical mask rule. I would go mask-less, of course, and I was prepared to be challenged. But I was lucky. Just a few seconds before I entered the shop, the marshal, who was guarding the entrance with his high viz jacket, had to leave his post, for some reason, maybe to sort out the trollies. That was my opportunity to slip into Morrison's without being asked, why I wasn't wearing a face mask.

Everyone else was wearing the face nappy, apart from a man with a motorbike helmet. Every shopkeeper I saw was wearing a mask. I felt sorry for them. Not only were they stuck in a useless and harmful mask for many hours a day, they also had to see faceless people all day long. What impact does that have on their mental health? A young lady helped me out at the self-checkout. She was also cleaning the surfaces of each counter, as soon as a customer was finished. Before I left, I took out a leaflet from my bag, and left it behind on the counter. She probably picked it up soon after and had a look at it...

That same day I was also at Aldi. They don't have a marshal guarding the entrance there. I left a couple of leaflets on the packing shelf and also at the hand-sanitizer stand. I've never actually seen anyone using the ugly goo. The bottles usually stand at the entrance of every shop. Their appearance is utterly revolting! I can understand why they're avoided—even by the maskers!

It is sad that whenever we are in public, wherever people gather, they are told not to show their face. The operators behind all of this want us to be faceless, inhumane, without individuality.

VOTING

After I learned that you can also give an empty voting ballot or 'spoil' it by adding a comment, to express that you are not pleased with any of the suggested candidates, that's what I decided to do.

As we arrived at the polling station, we were greeted by the now-commonplace plethora of 'warning posters' that adorned the walls, garishly reminding us of the mandatory wearing of face coverings. Well, we had none, and I was ready to face the challenge. Somewhat surprisingly, I was spared this eventuality as, once indoors and past the masked-up women who were there to supervise proceedings, none of them challenged us, although one of them did seem to glare at us in a reproving manner. To fill out the ballot, you had to either have your own pen or use a pencil which you didn't have to return—after all, it could be infected with corona. I placed a cross for a candidate from the Reform Party. All other suggestions were people from parties which had not done anything to restore our freedoms. Therefore, on two of the ballot papers I wrote: 'No to the vax pass' and 'Restore all freedoms!'

I could have slipped a White Rose leaflet along with the ballot papers into the ballot box, but I forgot to do so. On the other hand, maybe not doing so was better, because that way we could continue to remain anonymous. It may have been easy to find out who had put in the White Rose leaflet, as we might have been the only unmasked ones, and the same women, who were sitting there, watching us, might've been the ones who were going to do the counting...

On the way home we passed a pin-wall (an old shed where people put up posters and advertisements). Our flyer, which I had hung up there, had been taken down, along with the slander against Dr Coleman (which someone had put there as a response). But never mind, I hung up two more flyers. One entitled: 'One year is more than enough!' and the other one a warning of the covid 'vaccines'.

When did it become forbidden to express your own opinion? When have true facts become a crime? When did it become forbidden for others to think for themselves and to choose for themselves what and whom to believe?

CENSORSHIP

I used to comment on the Daily Telegraph website. For months it went alright. I was among many other commenters who were sceptical about how the government was handling things. There was the occasional bully among the commenters, who seemed to be working for the 77th brigade— but I never got blocked until recently. I had signed up for a new subscription with a new account, but after posting comments warning about the so-called covid vaccine, my comments were no longer visible for others. I noticed something was wrong when I stopped getting 'likes', and when I logged out from my account and went back to look, I realised that my comments had been blocked! I cancelled my subscription and forgot about it for a while. But when I logged into my other (older) account, the same happened with this account. It started off well, with me commenting and warning of the 'vaccine', and people's reactions were mostly positive. Then at one point I noticed that reactions weren't coming anymore. I logged out and saw that my comments were hidden. They had deleted my comments, leaving them visible only to me. This I found quite sinister. After that I soon cancelled my account once again.

I'm getting tired of it all, as it seems censorship is being notched up a gear on other platforms too. YouTube is constantly deleting videos that contain factual evidence, even when uttered by acknowledged experts. As soon as something is perceived as contradicting the government's narrative, it is silenced! That's why so many YouTubers have opened up accounts on alternative platforms, such as Odysee, Brandnewtube, Bitchute, Rummble and Banned.video. Earlier back last year, I posted a couple of videos where I talked about the lockdown. I also uploaded videos with doctors from California and Dr Carrie Madej who are opposed to the lockdowns or criticise the covid 'vaccine'. The videos with the doctors were soon deleted, sometimes even before having been published. I also received warnings from YouTube for 'violating their community rules'. Of course, non of my 'violations' were against any common sense rules, but these days, things have changed for the worse. No discussion is allowed, only con-formity with the brainwashing narrative of the government and the MSM (mainstream media). It is no coincidence, of course. This has been planned well ahead. In 2019 Big Tech and other major broadcasters and newspapers got together to agree on how to impose censorship.

7

Other White Rose Groups

We don't do stickers—and although it is stated on the website, I still sometimes get inquiries about stickers, in addition to complaints and threats. Once someone even said they'd sue us if we didn't remove the stickers by a certain date and we'd have to pay for the damage. I ignored the message, because it clearly says on the contact form page, that we don't do stickers and that we'd ignore emails regarding stickers. Who is doing the stickers? I can honestly say, I do not know these people. I do not know who started the group and where it all began. All I know is that, before our White Rose UK website was up, before we even purchased the domain, I did some research to find out if a White Rose group already existed in the UK. There was nothing there, so I went ahead. Some time later—probably after weeks or even months—a family member came up with an online poster featuring a group called White Rose, and it turned out they were distributing black and white stickers with anti-lockdown texts on them. They also wanted to remain strictly anonymous.

I found it intriguing that there is another group also called the White Rose modelled on the World War II German anti-Nazi underground resistance movement. Although we are independent of them, what unites both groups however, is that, like our heroic predecessors we are all fighting against tyranny and oppression. Although this time it is against 21st Century draconian covid legislation. We share the same goal. In the end, it's not about us, it's about the message we are sending out in to the world. In a certain way, we are continuing the work of the German freedom fighters. We embody the same spirit. It's not solely our work; I may call it the work of the Holy Spirit. The German White Rose pioneers might even be praying for us from heaven...

One day someone wrote to me and sent a link to a website entitled the White Rose Ireland. Together with others, she had only recently set up that website which includes a lot of medical information that opposes the covid propaganda. It was great news to see that the same thing was happening in another, nearby country. She later explained that they had come across the German White Rose on the internet for the first time and wondered, why they hadn't learned about this at school. Then they decided they needed to do something similar. First I thought they might have been inspired by our website. But the person who wrote to me mentioned that two weeks after their website was up, she discovered the White Rose UK website!

Another time a Dutchman asked me if he could use some of our website's content as he wished to do a White Rose website for Holland. Of course, I happily agreed. Currently, there are three White Rose websites listed under 'International' in the website's menu.

8

Poem—Don't Be Silenced

You tell the facts and you don't care
What others say or think.
People, who go out of their way and dare
Will not let this country sink.

You sit, stand or walk about
You talk calm, shout or sing
From your pub you kick politicians out
Traitors don't fit under your wing.

Unmasked on the train and in the shop
You put up with bullying and assault
But even if you lose your job
It's not your own fault.

The maskers look anxiously
Around the world they allowed
To turn that way through government lies
Deceits, to which they bowed.

You warriors give us hope and encouragement
Speak true science and common sense.
And when the day is far spent
Everyone will see through truth's lens.

For now, keep fighting, warrior
You don't have to be put to shame.
Don't succumb to covid terror
It's *they* who've gone insane.

9

Protests

Before taking part in the freedom march on 24 April 2021 I had already been to several protests. The first one I went to was possibly the first one that ever took place against covid restrictions, apart from a small protesting group around Piers Corbyn. On that day in May 2020, two family members and I arrived much too late at Hyde Park, but there were still protesters around, sitting on the grass, some talking to the police and some being sent home because they weren't abiding to the restrictions. There may have been around 200 people present. In contrast to this first protest, the April 2021 march consisted of hundreds of thousands participants!

In October 2020 there was a rally with around 45,000 people, and speeches were held. At the end of the rally a group of officers intervened and broke up a speech given by German doctor Heiko Schöning. As this happened, I wasn't fully aware of what was going on, because I was standing in the very back. All I noticed was some kind of unrest emerging with the arrival of the police. After the rally, the huge crowd marched up Oxford Street chanting things like 'take off the mask' and 'freedom'. Later on in Hyde Park ironically at Speakers' Corner, the same German doctor was arrested and placed in handcuffs (I only find that out later in a video).

Following all of this, subsequent protest taking place in London were like games of cat and mouse, as groups of protesters were repeatedly chased and dispersed by the roving police units. I witnessed several arrests of peaceful protesters, some of them were treated needlessly brutally by the police. Even a family member came under arrest, while peacefully strolling through the park, behind a group of protesters, and was kept in custody for a few hours. They took away 12 of our White Rose picket signs plus a box of business cards which had been packed in a rucksack. There had been no chance to lend the picket signs to anyone because the police had harangued us from the outset. Needless to say all the fines issued in this context were completely unlawful.

This is what I published on the website in November 2020:

Large groups of Protesters Chased and Harassed by Police

On Saturday, thousands of protesters gathered near Marble Arch protesting loudly against totalitarian CV19 restrictions and lockdowns.

The police presence was considerable. Dozens of police vans were driving around the city centre, hunting for protesters. Police on foot were splitting up groups, harassing and arresting people. Like a cat and mouse chase, the protesters were scattered all over the city centre whilst trying to regroup in new locations. The protest was meant to begin at Kings Cross, but police action made it impossible for anyone to gather there. Later the venue changed to Angels, then Marble Arch and Hyde Park, Speakers' Corner.

Police have been stopping people on the streets and telling them to go home. Many peaceful protesters were arrested simply for standing up for freedom. One member of the White Rose was also arrested, along with several others, while she happened to be strolling behind a group of marching protesters. Those arrested were taken into custody and kept there until evening. The police confiscated protest material. Police also issued fines. In several cases police were brutally manhandling protesters to the ground, inevitably hurting them, harass-

> *ing and violating their basic rights. This is pure fascism,
> and the UK has become a police state.*

Then things changed from March 2021. I could hardly believe it when I was watching online around 100,000 people marching through London and without police intervention. A month later, when we took part in a protest again, that number had increased. It was very uplifting to march in glorious weather, alongside so many like-minded, happy people fighting together for freedom. I was there with three family members and a woman whom we had met on a small protest, back in November.

My husband and I went on the Freedom March on 15th May. On the same day freedom rallies were taking place all across the globe. Tens of thousands were protesting in front of the BBC Broadcasting House, yet the BBC still failed to acknowledge it or to show any footage of it whatsoever in any of their news coverage! Another major London protest was on 29 May, where my husband and I attended and our friend. Several Tube stations near Parliament Square were closed on that day, which made it difficult to attend the march.

Large crowds filled up around the Churchill statue, and when the fireworks went off, the march began through the city centre.

I don't have any official numbers of how many people took part on that day, as the mainstream media chose to either ignore or distort the truth about the protest, but some say there could've be up to a million. Among the crowds were people from all walks of life. We discovered around three Catholic groups, some carrying a Mary statue, the Merciful Jesus image or a Guadalupe image, and praying the rosary. I spoke to a man who was carrying a flag with 'St David pray for us!' written on it. He had mentioned that we had passed the Tyburn Convent, and that the nuns had been waving to the protesters. Days after that, (on a video recording) one of the nuns was heard to say that people had been asking her to pray for 50 people who had died after the covid jab! The five hour march began at Parliament Square, passed the main shopping areas, and went all the way to London Acton, with residents waving from their doorsteps and windows.

10

It's All the Opposite of What They Say

Whatever happens, don't take the vaccine!
(A comment I made repeatedly before the roll-out of the
covid vaccines.)

They say you must wear a mask—not only to protect yourself, but to protect others. But masks are physically and mentally harmful, especially in the long term.

They say everyone should get the 'vaccine'—but they hide the deaths and severe side effects caused by this covid injection.

They say you need to keep testing to protect others—but the test swabs are contaminated with poison.

They said you could pass on covid even if you have no symptoms (so-called asymptomatic), but all they want is to push the numbers of 'cases' up and ramp up fear.

They say keep your distance out of care for others—but they are destroying us mentally by this kind of social engineering.

They say the virus is killing people—but the lockdowns have caused far more deaths.

They say you need to isolate in order to keep the virus under control—but that way we become more vulnerable for diseases.

They must know it because this has been going on for over a year now.

They said, lockdown will last three weeks to flatten the curve. Lockdowns and restrictions lasted over a year, and there's no end in sight.

They say you'll get your freedom back, but they want everyone to have a vaccine passport in order to control us even more.

They want us to believe in their new normal—but there's nothing normal about it.

Previously, they said any illness or symptom was due to covid, but when people now show side-effects or die after receiving the covid injection, they say the 'vaccine' is not the reason, it's just a coincidence.

Everything they say is the opposite of how it is.

They pretend they're telling the truth, but in fact they're lying in our face.

11

Depopulation

DID PRINCE PHILIP REALLY SAY THIS?

'In the event that I am reincarnated, I would like to return as a deadly virus, to contribute something to solving overpopulation.' (Philip, Duke of Edinburgh, 1988 to Deutsche Presse-Agentur)

Which leaves us with some questions... Was Prince Philip part of the depopulation agenda? Did he belong to an elite that wants to eliminate a great part of the human race? By saying 'solving overpopulation' who do they mean, and where would they begin?

Yes, may his soul rest in peace... But we need to fight against evil agendas!

(Published on thewhiterose.uk, 11/4/2021)

IS THIS WHAT'S DRIVING BORIS JOHNSON AND MEMBERS OF THE WEF?

Anyone who has done a little research throughout the past year has come across the plans of the Great Reset. They of course didn't emerge by accident or due to an unforeseen pandemic. The plans of the Great Reset, also known as One World Order, have been carefully planned decades ahead. Those who dig deeper, will soon find out that at the core of this manufactured crisis, it's all about depopulation.

A tiny minority of the world population have come to the conclusion, that we are too many on this earth and that a great lot of the too many should be removed. And they have been spreading the myth for decades, despite the fact that there is food and space enough for the entire population. The real issue is not that we are too many, but that people have been moved from the country-side into cramped cities, and that 1% of the population, own far too much for themselves. It is the same 'elite' that is responsible for the greatest fraud in history.

But who are the too many? Who do they want to get rid of? Do they mean their own families (bear in mind that Boris Johnson is father of at least six children)? Probably not! Even if there were such a thing as 'overpopulation'—what would give them the right to decide which lives are worth sustaining and which ones not? Haven't we learned from history yet? It seems they haven't.

They had to come up with a plan. How about letting fear and vaccination do the job? Use a virus to create a pandemic, perhaps, which frightens everyone out of their wits? Then give them the vaccination as a cure, which eventually, will help 'reduce population'? How about beginning with the eld-erly, the fragile and vulnerable, how about making people in-fertile?

In his blog, back in 2007, the now Prime Minister Boris Johnson wrote an article called Global Population Control. You may find some clues into what is driving him and his ilk to inflict so much pain and calumny to human society.

(Published on thewhiterose.uk, 25/5/2021)

12

Leafleting

Family members and I as well as countless others have been distributing leaflets since the first one was distributed in September 2020. We began with handing them out on the streets and leaving them behind on busses and trains. Later we put them through people's doors, hung them up on pin boards or left them in shops and other public places.

On one occasion our local newsletter outlet, in a direct challenge to our work, printed an image of one of the leaflets that we had hung on the wooden wall at the bus stop. The title of the article said something about misinformation. They wrote a whole page about the 'scandalous' leaflet, warning about a group called the White Rose that was spreading 'life-threatening misinformation'. Those who wrote the article claimed to be virologists and offered their contact details for readers eager to learn more, whilst at the same time they encouraged immediate vaccine take-up. In reality, much like the Nazis in World War II did, in order to promulgate the state's skewed narrative, they simply sought to undermine any legitimate criticism or opposition. Indeed, in line with the government propaganda machine, such people seek to scare the meek into compliance, and to silence and oppose any contrary voice, not allowing people to think for themselves. The irony of all this is, while labelling us dangerous, they don't notice how dangerous they are; they aim to suppress the warnings of doctors, professors, microbiologists and virologists who warn of the dangers of the covid jab (a 'vaccine' that will alter people's DNA and kill them) instead, urging readers to comply and take the 'vaccine'.

I wonder if they're aware that by not listening to their own conscience and blindly following the government propaganda, one day they will be brought to justice? Are they so brainwashed that they don't realise how they are supporting a dystopian society ruled by liars and murderers?

The 'war' against the leaflets didn't end there. After I had hung up another leaflet on a pin wall, a family member came across a post in a local online group. Someone called our leaflet 'a nonsense', but instead of ripping it down had added to their comments a copied extract from Wikipedia—a slanderous article besmirching the renowned and respected Dr Vernon Coleman. (In a video recording Dr Coleman said that after having made his first video at the beginning of the corona fraud, his Wikipedia entry had been deliberately tampered with in order to undermine his credibility.) Interestingly, no mention was made of the similar claims by the other eminent doctors and scientists or indeed that of acclaimed lawyer Dr Reiner Füllmich. What a nasty and underhand way to undermine a genuine and urgent warning about the life threatening so-called vaccines! Clearly, those who would stoop to such tactics do not accept the principles of free speech or the freedom of people to be permitted to hold their own opinions or to decide for themselves who or what to believe in.

On the other hand, by observing the White Rose being placed in a bad light, there is the hope that some readers might take comfort in the knowledge that there is a resistance movement out there after all.

One time, I received an email from a lady who informed me that thanks to overhearing some people complaining about leaflets in her locality, she discovered the White Rose. As a result, by contacting me she was thereafter able to meet other like-minded people.

Some run after us, after getting the leaflet, to express their gratitude. Others run after us to insult and swear. These are truly testing days. In one of the original White Rose leaflets from the German resistance group it said. 'We will not keep silent, we are your guilty conscience; the White Rose will not leave you in peace!' And this speaks for us today.

13

The White Rose UK Leaflets

LEAFLET I

A CONTINUATION OF THE WHITE ROSE 2020
'... AND THEIR SPIRIT STILL LIVES ON'

In the midst of World War II a German underground movement called the White Rose distributed leaflets calling on people to passively resist the Nazi regime.

The reasons for this were the tyranny of the Nazis in Europe and the restrictions on freedom in Germany. The siblings Scholl and their comrades, whose beliefs were rooted in the Christian faith, emphasised the importance of freedom for individuals, independent of their cultural background. They recognised the ongoing dictatorship of Hitler as a force coming from the evil one.

The third flyer stated that every single human is entitled to a practical government that guarantees the freedom of every single person and the wellbeing of the community. Every human should be able to reach their natural goal, their earthly joy, autonomously and by their own accord. The White Rose spoke to their conscience and urged people to wake up from their dangerous lethargy.

Even though we are not suffering from a lack of food or the danger of bombs dropping on our homes, there are remarkable parallels in the White Rose's appeal to the current coronavirus crisis. In several countries in Europe and around the world we have been brainwashed into panic over a virus from which the vast majority of people will not get ill, yet alone die of. Listen to the experts—doctors, professors, virologists and epidemiologists—who explain why the lockdown is pointless. We have always lived with viruses and we will need to live with this one too.

Covid-19 is not more dangerous than a bad flu. The way it's being handled, the disproportionate and dehumanising restrictions and rules, is a disgrace to humanity. People protesting against the lockdown have been arrested like criminals for gathering and exercising their right of free speech.

At the same time, Youtube and Facebook censor videos and posts that do not match the current trend of the mainstream media. If you publish scientific facts, interviews or a philosophical approach opposed to lockdown, your video or post may quickly be taken down.

In England it has become compulsory to wear a face mask on public transport, similar to other countries that brought this in a few weeks before, such as Poland, where you can be fined up to 30,000 złoty for not wearing a mask. For some, this could mean two years' wages just for not wearing a mask in public! The mask itself is useless and even dangerous, due to a reduced influx of oxygen as well as bacteria collecting on the material. Some overly-influenced people believe it's necessary to wear a mask, not only on public transport, but also when shopping or riding on their bike. Have you ever thought of this: the mask is a symbol of submission that muzzles us.

The lockdown has kept millions of people under house arrest for the past few months. But it's not over yet. In the UK the government has introduced a Track and Trace system. If you show symptoms of coronavirus, you will need to do a test and then go into quarantine. You will also have to report all people you have come in close contact with. Your and their data will be stored. Why has there been so much emphasis on data protection recently, when the violation of privacy is happening right now, in front of our eyes? This new system will require 25,000 people to deal with the data. In Italy people are being engaged to watch folks practice social distance behaviour. Doesn't this remind you of what they called denunciating during Stasi days?

Don't you see, it's all about control! The Track and Trace system is not obligatory yet, but may become so, as the Prime Minister himself stated. Same with the mobile-phone app, which you are told to download when crossing the border into the UK. Similar orders are given in other countries. How can we resist? By not testing and not exposing friends and family; by not downloading the corona app and by leaving the phone at home or using a phone without apps. If we don't want our freedom to slip away, we must resist.

People travelling into the UK are now forced to fill out an online form with their data and must stay in quarantine for two weeks. If they refuse, they face fines of £100 and £1000. In Germany, pubs and restaurants must ask their visitors to leave their data behind after 'enjoying' a series of social distance rules during their stay. In reality, there is nothing social about these rules. They are anti-social. It's inevitable that this will have a negative impact on society's social and mental well-being.

Will this crisis eventually lead to forced vaccination? There is no proof that a vaccination helps. Several doctors mention that you are better off without it. There is also talk about a microchip which would be implanted through vaccination. This microchip is not fantasy, it already exists. Do you really want to be chipped and have your life monitored? Do you want a global totalitarian state to control your life? It's up to you and me to say no to mandatory vaccination and chipping, and to end this global terror!

Bit by bit we have given up our freedom and our natural rights out of fear of a virus. Even though there is now enough evidence that coronavirus is not more dangerous than influenza, certain rights are taken from us and may not be given back easily. Our economy will suffer from severe damage and poverty will increase. How many people have lost their job and how many businesses are ruined? Have you thought of the raised taxes we will have to pay in the coming years so the government can pay off debts? And all along there's this question in the background: is this all intentional, are we dealing with a planned-demic, rather than a pandemic?

Since the weekly clapping ritual for the NHS has ceased, it's time to wake up from your sleep-walk and to realise what has happened to our freedom. The so-called 'new normal' is not normal, it's entirely abnormal. Never get used to it! It's time to take over responsibility and to make decisions for ourselves, or else the next generation of grown-ups will not experience the same freedom we've had before corona.

Some schools are opening in June, but have you observed the new distancing rules? Keeping children constantly at a distance of two metres in class and on school grounds is unreasonable and dehumanising, and will have a damaging impact on children's mental development. Parents should now resist such guinea-pig methods. It's not the way we grew up, and we should make sure our children grow up with the same freedoms we enjoyed.

Just as the White Rose called people to passively resist, this is what we need to do now. It is time to end the lockdown and social distancing. It is time to visit friends and family, the lonely, the vulnerable and the dying. It's time to admit that we are humans and not controllable robots. We need natural social interaction, without anti-social distancing and without face masks. If we all go about and live our life, ignoring social distance rules, those who want to control us will eventually have to give up.

Journalists, teachers, doctors, lawyers, politicians—stand up for the truth and speak publicly; be a voice for the voiceless and the silenced! If the majority of us rid ourselves of fear and panic and make use of common sense, we will be able to guarantee a future of peace and freedom for our children and grandchildren. To do so is not just a right, it's our moral duty!

This Continuation of the White Rose is not a copy of the communications of the resistance movement in 1942, where people paid with their life for their brave actions; however, the Continuation of the White Rose is an appeal driven by the same spirit; a spirit descending from the conscience, which rises up against injustice; a spirit nurtured by the depth of the heart where truth is embedded.

Aristotle wrote in 'About Politics':

'... further it belongs (to the nature of tyrants) that nothing stays hidden, what a subject says or does, but everywhere spies overhear them ... further to inflame everyone and friends to fall out with each other and the nation with the noble and rich among each other. Thereafter, to such tyrannously measures it belongs to make the subjects poor, so that the bodyguards can be salaried, so that they are worried with the daily purchase and don't have time and leisure to incite any plot ... further also such high income taxes, as Syracuse imposed, because under Dionysus the citizens of this state happily spent their whole fortune. And also, the tyrant tends to constantly provoke wars ...'

(from the third leaflet of the German White Rose).

Please copy and distribute!

(Pentecost, 31 May 2020)

LEAFLET 2

WE HAVE BEEN TRICKED INTO A GLOBAL SCAM. LET'S END IT NOW!

The message 'save lives', that the government is using to justify lockdowns and other restrictions is a gross misrepresentation of the facts:

• For most people covid-19 is no more dangerous than the flu. In fact, 99.8% of those who contract the virus will survive it.

• The average age at death of those dying with covid-19 is above 82 years—greater than the average life expectancy in the UK!

• Of those who died with covid-19, most had a serious pre-existing condition which was most likely the cause of death.

Despite these facts the government and the mainstream media have orchestrated a campaign of fear misleading the people, frightening us into believing we are in the midst of the deadliest pandemic ever, forcing us to accept restrictions on our liberty and accept unproven and untested vaccines to 'beat the virus' and 'save the NHS'. What is happening in the background is a silent genocide.

More people will die from the restrictions and lockdowns than from the virus.

• Hospitals have been emptied for covid-19 patients that never turned up.

• Treatments for other patients have been delayed or cancelled.

• Thousands of excess deaths will result from undiagnosed und untreated conditions.

Lockdowns lead to:

• loneliness and depression, a surge in mental health problems and increase of suicides

• disruption of education and loss of opportunities for young people

• closure of countless businesses

• loss of employment and livelihoods

Mandating the wearing of masks does nothing to 'beat the virus'. There is no study that proves that masks are effective in reducing the transmission of any virus in a community setting. Masks:

• reduce oxygen and increase CO_2 intake

• impair cognitive function

• can cause respiratory illnesses and oral infections

Masks are dehumanising and are a symbol of suppression and control.

Fear, lockdowns, masks, social distancing and control are all efforts by governments to get people to accept the new vaccine. A vaccine considered dangerous by many experts around the world.

It's all part of the globalist Great Reset, also known as New World Order.
Governments who are adapting to the Great Reset are trying to mandate the vaccine by using methods of coercion or exclusion for those refusing to accept it. This is against interna-

tional law!

It is time to stop this global crime on humanity!

Please copy and distribute. Visit thewhiterose.uk for more information.

(Created in December 2020)

LEAFLET 3

ONE YEAR IS MORE THAN ENOUGH!
(CHURCH LEAFLET)

• One year of entering and leaving church without blessed water.

• One year without communal singing—'He who sings, prays twice!' (St. Augustine).

• One year of shortened liturgy at Mass and months without any Mass at all.

• One year without receiving Communion in the mouth.

• One year with every second bench barred and fewer attendees than before.

• One year of dodgy hand sanitizer instead of blessed water.

• One year of cult-like mask wearing.

• One year of guards controlling church visitors, as if they were prisoners.

• One year without prayer groups, Bible meetings, youth and children's groups.

• One year without socialising after Church.

• One year of screens instead of real meetings.

• One year without (or with restricted) weddings, funerals, Baptism, First Communion and Confirmation.

• One year of separation from the elderly, the vulnerable, and those in need of charity.

• One year without collecting cash donations (in order for us to get used to a cashless society).

• Do you know that you have been lied to for over a year?

• Do you know that there is no real pandemic (the first lockdown was only meant to last 3 weeks)?

• Do you know that very few die of covid (average age of death is 82; and there are many incorrect death records)?

• Do you know that far more people are dying due to lockdowns and restrictions than from the virus?

• Do you know that masks are useless and bad for your physical and mental health?

• Do you know that more people die of the seasonal flu than of covid (the rebranded 'flu')?

• Do you know that test and trace is a preliminary practice for an unlawful vaccination pass?

• Do you know that the covid test is useless and produces mainly false positives?

• Do you know that the 'vaccine' is an experimental gene therapy for killing and changing mankind?

• Do you know that the Church has given up so much for nothing?

• Do not wait for the government to give back your religious freedom—they don't want to, ever!

• God is above the Church, not the government; the Church is responsible before Him in first place!

• It is time to stand up for our religious freedom, for free speech and charity (enough of virtue signalling)!

• It is the Church's duty to expose this biggest global fraud in history; this is a fight against evil!

• We must put an end to the depopulation, 'agenda 21' plan. Lives are depending on this.

• It is time to get on our knees and pray that our faith becomes strong again!

• In the name of God, let us fight for our faith—if we lose our faith we will lose everything.

Resources

1. Did you know that we are all exempt from wearing a mask? See under the title: 'When you do not need to wear a face covering' on the government website (gov.uk/government/publications/face-covering-s-when-to-wear-one-and-how-to-make-your-own/face-coverings-when-to-wear-one-and-how-to-make-your-own) where it says: '...to avoid harm or injury, or the risk of harm or injury, to yourself or others'. Masks harm everyone (over the short or long-term), therefore we are all exempt.

2. Did you know that the government officially downgraded the status of covid on the 19 March 2020? On the government website it says: 'As of 19 March 2020, covid-19 is no longer considered to be a high consequence infectious disease (HCID) in the UK.' (gov.uk/guidance/high-consequence-infectious-diseases-hcid)

3. Learn more about the deadly, so-called vaccine: thewhiterose.uk/category/vaccination

4. Please do not throw this leaflet away, read it, talk about it, share it and save lives. Have you done your research? Visit: thewhiterose.uk

(Created in April 2021)

LEAFLET 4

DO YOU HAVE DOUBTS ABOUT THE SCIENCE BEHIND THIS GLOBAL PANDEMIC?

Who is dying of covid?

For most people covid-19 is no more dangerous than the flu. 99.8% of those who contract the virus survive it. The average age at death of those dying with covid-19 is above 82 years —greater than the average life expectancy in the UK. Of those who have covid-19 on their death record, the majority had at least one pre-existing condition which was most likely the cause of their death.

What is the result of lockdowns and restrictions?

Hospitals have been emptied for covid-19 patients that never turned up. Treatments for other patients have been delayed or cancelled. Tens of thousands of excess deaths will result from undiagnosed and untreated conditions. Lockdowns lead to loneliness and depression, a surge in mental health problems and suicides, the disruption of education, the loss of opportunities for young people, the closure of countless businesses and the loss of employment and livelihoods. As a result, more people are dying from the restrictions and lockdowns than from the virus. Was this deliberate?

What is the point of wearing a mask?

There is no study that proves that masks are effective in reducing the transmission of any virus in a community setting. Instead, masks reduce oxygen and increase the CO_2 intake, impair cognitive function, and can cause respiratory illnesses, oral infections, skin problems and brain damage. The masks are a dehumanising symbolic tool for suppression and control.

Are covid vaccines safe?

Doubts have been raised as to the safety of some vaccines and use has been restricted for certain age groups. Several countries have suspended some vaccines pending further examination. Reports of increased deaths in care homes following vaccinations have begun to surface as well as reports of extreme adverse side effects. The currently approved covid-19 vaccinations are still experimental and have only been approved under emergency provisions. Full long-term trial results for these are not due until 2023. The manufacturers point out that the vaccines do not confer immunity and that it is still possible to contract covid having been vaccinated and that mask wearing and social distancing must still be observed. Given all that we don't know about these 'vaccines', and that people are dying having been vaccinated, are we witnessing a silent genocide?

Do we need a vaccine certification or vaccine passport?

If you have read the above, you will understand that a vaccine pass is not only unnecessary, it is also a gross violation of our freedom and our right of movement. We should never let it happen!

'Three weeks to flatten the curve', they said. It's been now over a year of lockdowns and restrictions. And with the announcement of further years of mask wearing and social distancing—bad for our physical, mental and societal health—**there's no end in sight**.

We must stop this global crime on humanity! Please copy and distribute. Spread the truth and save lives. Have you done your research? Visit thewhiterose.uk

(Created in April 2021)

LEAFLET 5

ONE YEAR IS MORE THAN ENOUGH!
(STREET HANDOUT)

Do you know that you have been lied to for over a year (remember '3 weeks to flatten the curve')?

Do you know that there is no real pandemic? *

Do you know that very few die of covid? (The average age of death is 82, and there are many false death records.)

Do you know that far more people are dying due to lockdowns and restrictions than from the virus?

Do you know that masks are useless and bad for your physical and mental health? **

Do you know that more people die of the seasonal flu than of covid (which is now the rebranded 'flu')?

Do you know that test and trace is a preliminary practice for an unlawful vaccination pass/certificate?

Do you know that the covid test is useless and produces mainly false positives?

Do you know that the 'vaccine' is an experimental gene therapy for killing and changing mankind?

Don't wait for the corrupt globalist governments to give back our freedom—they don't want to, ever!

This is a war against the people. Let's end this silent genocide, and defend our freedom and humanity!

 * Check out on government website where it says: 'As of 19 March 2020, covid-19 is no longer considered to be a high consequence infectious disease in the UK.'

 ** See under the title: 'When you do not need to wear a face covering' on the government website where it says: '…to avoid harm or injury, or the risk of harm or injury, to yourself or others'. Masks harm everyone (over the short or long-term), therefore we are all exempt.

Have you done your research? Visit: thewhiterose.uk and join the resistance!

Share this leaflet and save lives.

(Created in April 2021)

LEAFLET 6

AN URGENT WARNING—
COVID 'VACCINE' IS THREATENING HUMANITY

The Government and the mainstream media are not telling the truth, that is why grass-root movements are now doing the job. We were 750,000 protesting in London on Saturday 24 April 2021, and we are growing in numbers!

Read what renowned experts say below. There are many more experts from all around the world warning us about the worst genocide humanity will have ever witnessed.

You may or may not have experience side effects after vaccination. But they will possibly appear later, and many people have already died after the jab.

• Dr Sucharit Bhakdi, microbiologist: '**They are killing people with covid vaccines to reduce the world's population.**'

• Dr Mike Yeadon, former Pfizer Vice President: '**That pathway will be used for mass depopulation.**'

• Dr Geer Vanden Bossche phD, Gates top virologist: '**The vaccines are threatening humanity. They should be cancelled immediately.**'

• Professor Dolores Cahill: '**This mRA vaccine is killing people.**'

• Dr Coleman: '**The covid jab causes infertility.**'

• Dr Carrie Madej: '**They want to change our DNA.**'

• Dr Reiner Fuellmich, German top lawyer: '**Those responsible for the corona fraud scandal must be criminally prosecuted for crimes against humanity.**'

• NHS Board Level Whistleblower: '**We are causing genocide.**'

• MHRA Yellow Card (19/5/2021): **1,213 deaths, 859,481 adverse reactions** from covid jab in the UK (only an est. 10% have been reported)

Please do not dismiss this warning. Share it and save lives! Wake up before it's too late!

Type in the names above and read or listen to full interviews and talks on thewhiterose.uk

(April/May 2021)

LEAFLET 7

END THE COVID FRAUD AND GLOBAL GENOCIDE NOW!

People are experiencing serious adverse reactions after receiving the covid jab, or are dying. Many more will die in the coming months and years. The covid fraud is causing a global genocide. This needs to end now. These are the crimes being committed or supported by governments, government advisory groups, members of the World Economic Forum, the mainstream media, social media platforms and other agencies in positions of authority:

• Extreme fear mongering via press releases, media announcements and nation-wide advertisement, using taxpayers' money.

• Inducing unnecessary fear and terror of a virus less lethal than a strong seasonal flu.

• Cynical use of new variants to promote fear and justify continued restrictions.

• Falsifying death records by stating covid as the primary cause of death when not applicable.

• Mask mandates on public transport, in shops, schools, work places and other public places—in many cases for hours a day —exposing the wearer to potential and actual damage to their mental and physical well-being.

• Forcing children and adults to take covid tests, often regularly, that are not fit for purpose, produce mainly false positives, and can cause damage to health.

• Using covid 'cases', which are based on false test results, for prolonging covid restrictions and lockdowns.

• Coercing people into taking an experimental 'vaccine', which is in fact a gene-modifying injection, can induce infertility, and is causing more adverse reactions and deaths than all other vaccines together.

• Promoting the use of an unlicensed 'vaccine' as though it were fully approved and safe.

• Suppressing or underplaying the data regarding adverse reactions and deaths of the covid jabs.

• Ignoring the Nuremberg Code by not enabling people to give informed consent before vaccination or testing.

• Disruption of education.

• Suppression of religious freedom, prevention of worship.

• Restricting freedom of movement across borders, and during lockdowns, within the country.

• Causing job losses, business failures and loss of opportunities.

• Delaying diagnosis and treatment of conditions far more serious than covid resulting in unnecessary loss of life.

• Forced quarantine of healthy people at their own expense.

• Suppression of the right to protest, freedom of association and freedom of speech.

• Suppression of scientific debate, giving voice only to 'approved' agencies.

Find out more: thewhiterose.uk

(Created in June 2021)

14

English Translations of
the German White Rose Leaflets

FIRST LEAFLET (1942)

Leaflets of the White Rose.

I

Nothing is more unworthy of a cultural people than to be 'governed' without resistance by an irresponsible clique of rulers who surrender to dark urges. Is it not the case that every honest German today is ashamed of his government, and who of us foresees the extent of the disgrace that will come upon us and our children once the veil has fallen from our eyes and the most atrocious crimes, infinitely exceeding all measure, come to light? If the German people are already so corrupted and decayed in their deepest being that they, without lifting a hand, in reckless trust in a questionable law of history, give away the highest thing that a human being possesses and that elevates him above every other creature, namely free will, if the Germans, so devoid of any individuality, have already become so much a mindless and cowardly mass, then, yes, then they deserve their downfall.

Goethe speaks of the Germans as a tragic people, like that of the Jews and Greeks, but today it seems

77

rather as if they were a shallow, will-less herd of hangers-on, from which the marrow is sucked out of the innermost and who, now deprived of their core, are ready to be rushed to ruin. It seems so—but it is not so; rather, in a slow, deceptive, systematic rape, each individual has been put into a spiritual prison, and only when he lay bound in it did he become aware of the doom. Only a few recognized the impending doom, and the reward for their heroic admonition was death. The fate of these people will be discussed later.

If everyone waits for the others to begin, the messengers of the avenging nemesis will inexorably draw nearer and nearer, then even the last victim will be thrown senselessly into the jaws of the insatiable demon. Therefore, each individual, conscious of his responsibility as a member of the Christian and occidental culture, must in this last hour resist as much as he can, work against the scourge of humanity, against fascism and every system of the absolute state similar to it. Offer passive resistance—r e s i s t a n c e—wherever you are, prevent the further running of this atheistic war machine before it is too late, before the last cities are a heap of ruins, like Cologne, and before the last youth of the people somewhere has bled to death for the hubris of a subhuman. Do not forget that every people deserves the government it can bear!

From Friedrich Schiller, 'The Legislation of Lycurgus and Solon':

'... Held against its own purpose, the legislation of

Lycurgus is a masterpiece of statecraft and philanthropy. He wanted a powerful state, founded in itself, indestructible; political strength and permanence were the ends to which he aspired, and this end he attained as far as was possible under his circumstances. But if one holds the purpose which Lycurgus set before himself against the purpose of mankind, a deep disapproval must take the place of the admiration which the first fleeting glance has won from us. Everything may be sacrificed to the best of the state, except that to which the state itself serves only as a means. The state itself is never an end, it is only important as a condition under which the end of mankind can be fulfilled, and this end of mankind is no other than the training of all of man's powers, progress. If a state constitution hinders the development of all the powers that lie in man; if it hinders the progress of the spirit, it is reprehensible and harmful, however well thought-out and perfect in its nature it may be. Its permanence itself is then much more a reproach than a glory—it is then only a prolonged evil; the longer it endures, the more harmful it is.

... At the expense of all moral feelings political merit was gained and the ability to do so was trained. In Sparta there was no conjugal love, no maternal love, no filial love, no friendship there was nothing but citizenship, nothing but civic virtue.

... A state law made it the duty of the Spartans to be inhuman to their slaves; in these unhappy victims of slaughter, humanity was insulted and maltreated. In the Spartan code itself the dangerous principle was preached to regard human beings as means and not as ends, thus the foundations of natural law and morality were lawfully torn down.

... What more beautiful spectacle gives the rough warrior Gaius Marcius in his camp before Rome, who sacrifices revenge and victory, because he cannot see the
tears of the mother flowing!'

'... The state (of Lycurgus) could continue only on the
single condition that the spirit of the people should
stand still; it could therefore preserve itself only
by failing the highest and only purpose of a state.'

From Goethe's 'Awakening of Epimenides,' second
act, fourth performance:

Genii

.....

But what has boldly risen from the abyss,
Can by a brazen fate
Half the circle of the world surmount,
Yet it must return to the abyss.
Already a tremendous fear threatens,
In vain he will resist!
And all who still cling to him,
Must perish with it.

Hope

Now I meet my braves,
Who in the night are gathered together,
To be silent, not to sleep,
And the beautiful word of freedom

Is lisped and stammered,
Till in unaccustomed newness
We at our temple steps
Again rapturously call it:
  (With conviction, loudly:)
Freedom!
        (more moderate:)
        Freedom!
  (from all sides and ends echo:)
            Freedom!

We ask you to copy this sheet with as many tracing papers as possible and to distribute it further!

SECOND LEAFLET OF THE WHITE ROSE (1942)

Leaflets of the White Rose

II

One cannot deal with National Socialism spiritually, because it is unspiritual. It is wrong to speak of a National Socialist world view, because if it existed, one would have to try to prove or to fight it by intellectual means—but reality offers us a completely different picture: already in its first sprout this movement depended on the deception of fellow men, already then it was rotten to the core and could save itself only by the constant lie.

Yet Hitler himself writes in an early edition of 'his' book (a book written in the worst German I have ever read; yet it has been elevated to the status of the Bible by the people of poets and thinkers): 'One does not believe how one must deceive a people in order to govern them.' If this cancer of the German people had not yet made itself too noticeable at the beginning, it was only because there were still good enough forces at work to hold it back.

But as it grew bigger and bigger and finally came to power by means of a last mean corruption, the cancer broke open, as it were, and sullied the whole body, the majority of the former opponents hid themselves, the German intelligence took refuge in a cellar hole, in order to gradually suffocate there as a nightshade growth, hidden from the light and the sun. Now we are facing the end. Now it is important to find each other again, to enlighten each other from person to person, to always think about it and not to give each other any rest until even the last one is convinced of the utmost necessity of his fight against this system. If such a wave of revolt goes through the country, if 'it is in the air', if many join in, then in a last, tremendous effort this system can be shaken off. An end with horror is still better than horror without end.

It is not given to us to make a final judgment about the meaning of our history. But if this catastrophe is to serve us for salvation, then only in this way: to be purified by suffering, to long for the light out of the deepest night, to pick ourselves up and finally help to shake off the yoke that oppresses the world.

We do not want to write about the Jewish question in this paper, we do not want to write a defence speech —no, only as an example we want to briefly mention the fact, the fact that since the conquest of Poland three hundred thousand Jews have been murdered in this country in the most bestial way. Here we see the most terrible crime against the dignity of man, a crime that cannot be equalled by any other in the whole history of mankind. The Jews, too, are human beings—one may take whatever position one likes on the Jewish question—and such crimes were committed against human beings. Perhaps someone says that the Jews deserved such a fate; this assertion would be a tremendous presumption; but supposing someone said this, what is his attitude to the fact that the entire Polish aristocratic youth has been destroyed (God grant that it has not yet been!)?

In what way, you ask, has such a thing happened? All male offspring of noble families between 15 and 20 years of age were taken to concentration camps in Germany for forced labour, all girls of the same age were taken to Norway to the brothels of the SS! Why do we tell you all this, since you already know it yourself, if not these, then other equally serious crimes of terrible sub-humanity? Because here a question is touched upon which concerns us all deeply and which m u s t give us all food for thought. Why do the German people behave so apathetically in the face of all these most atrocious and inhuman crimes? Hardly anyone thinks about it. The fact is accepted as such and put aside. And again the German people sleep on in their dull, stupid sleep, giving these fascist criminals courage and opportunity to go on killing—and they do.

Should this be a sign that the Germans are brutalized in their most primitive human feelings, that no chord in them cries out shrilly in the face of such deeds, that they have sunk into a deadly sleep from which there is no awakening, never, ever? It seems so, and it certainly is, if the German does not finally rise from this stupor, if he does not protest wherever he can against this criminal clique, if he does not sympathize with these hundreds of thousands of victims. And not only does he have to feel pity, no, much more: c o m p l i c i t y . Because by his apathetic behaviour he only gives the possibility to these dark people to act in such a way, he suffers this 'government' which has loaded such an infinite guilt on itself, yes, he is nevertheless himself to blame for the fact that it could originate at all!

Everybody wants to absolve himself from such complicity, everybody does it and then sleeps again with the calmest, best conscience. But he cannot absolve himself, everyone is g u i l t y , g u i l t y , g u i l t y ! But it is not too late to get rid of this most abominable of all abominations of governments, in order not to load still more guilt on oneself. Now that our eyes have been fully opened in recent years, now that we know who we are dealing with, it is high time to eradicate this brown horde. Until the outbreak of the war, most of the German people were blinded, the National Socialists did not show themselves in their true form, but now that they have been recognized, it must be the only and highest duty, indeed the holiest duty of every German, to exterminate these beasts.

'He whose administration is inconspicuous, the people are glad. He whose administration is obtrusive, the people are broken. Misery, alas, is what happiness is built upon. Happiness, alas, only disguises misery. Where is this going to end? The end is not in sight. The orderly turns into disorder, the good turns into bad. The people are getting into confusion. Is it not so, daily, for a long time? Therefore, the Tall Man is rectangular, but he does not bump, he is angular, but does not hurt, he is upright, but not abrupt. He is clear, but does not want to shine.'

Lao-Tse.

• • • • •

'He who undertakes to dominate the empire
and shape it according to his will; I do not
see him achieving his goal; that is all.'
'The empire is a living organism; it cannot
be made, verily! He who wants to make it,
spoils it; he who wants to seize it, loses it.'
Therefore: 'Of the beings, some go ahead, others follow them; some breathe warmly, some
coldly; some are strong, some weak; some attain fullness, others succumb.'
'The High Man, therefore, refrains from ex-
aggeration, refrains from exaltation, refrains from encroachment.'

Lao-Tse.

· · · · ·

We ask that you copy and distribute this script- with
as many copies as possible.

THIRD LEAFLET OF THE WHITE ROSE (1942)

Leaflets of the White Rose

III

'Salus publica suprema lex.' [The public supreme law]

All ideal forms of state are utopias. A state cannot be constructed purely theoretically; it must grow, mature, just as the individual human being does. But it must not be forgotten that at the beginning of every culture there was the preliminary form of the state. The family is as old as man himself, and from this initial togetherness the rational man has created for himself a state, the foundation of which is to be justice and the highest law of which is to be the good of all. The state is to be an analogy of the divine order, and the highest of all utopias, the civitas Dei, is the model to which it is ultimately to approach. We do not wish to pass judgment here on the various possible forms of state, democracy, constitutional monarchy, kingship, etc. Only one thing wants to be emphasized clearly and unambiguously: every single human being has a right to a useful and just state, which secures the freedom of the individual as well as the welfare of the whole. For, according to God's will, man should seek to attain his natural goal, his earthly happiness in independence and self-activity, freely and independently in the coexistence and co-operation of the state community.

But our present 'state' is the dictatorship of evil. 'We have known this for a long time,' I hear you object, 'and we do not need this to be held up to us here again.' But, I ask you, if you know this, why do you not stir, why do you tolerate that these rulers, step by step, openly and covertly, rob one domain of your right after another, until one day nothing, but nothing at all, will be left but a mechanized state gear, commanded by criminals and drunkards? Has your mind already succumbed so much to rape that you forget that it is not only your right but your m o r a l d u t y to eliminate this system?

But if a man no longer musters the strength to demand his right, then he must perish with absolute necessity. We would deserve to be scattered all over the world like dust before the wind if we did not pick ourselves up in this twelfth hour and finally muster the courage that we have lacked since then. Do not hide your cowardice under the cloak of wisdom. Because with every day that you still hesitate, since you do not resist this spawn of hell, your guilt grows higher and higher like a parabolic curve.

Many, perhaps most, of the readers of these sheets are not clear about how to resist. They do not see any possibilities. We want to try to show them that everyone is able to contribute to the overthrow of this system. It is not through individualistic opposition, in the manner of bitter hermits, that it will be possible to make the ground ripe for an overthrow of this 'government' or even to bring about the overthrow as soon as possible, but only through the cooperation of many convinced, energetic people, people who agree on the means by which they can achieve their goal. We do not have a rich choice of such means, only one is available to us—p a s s i v e   r e s i s t a n c e.

The purpose and aim of passive resistance is to bring down National Socialism, and in this struggle we must not shrink from any path, from any deed, be they in any field. National Socialism must be attacked at a l l points where it can be attacked. An end must be put to this unstate as soon as possible—a victory of fascist Germany in this war would have <u>un</u>foreseeable, terrible consequences. Not the military victory over Bolshevism must be the first concern of every German, but the defeat of the National Socialists. This must <u>necessarily</u> come first. We shall prove to you the greater necessity of this last demand in one of our next papers.

And now every resolute opponent of National Socialism must put to himself the question: How can he fight against the present 'state' most effectively, how can he inflict it with the most sensitive blows? Through passive resistance—undoubtedly. It is clear that it is impossible for us to give guidelines for each individual's behaviour; we can only give general indications; everyone must find the path to realization himself.

S a b o t a g e in armament and war factories, sabotage in all meetings, rallies, festivities, organizations brought into being by the National Socialist Party. Preventing the smooth running of the war machine (a machine that works o n l y for a war that is solely about saving and preserving the National Socialist Party and its dictatorship). S a b o t a g e in all scientific and intellectual fields working for a continuation of the present war—be it in universities, colleges, laboratories, research institutes, technical offices. S a b o t a g e in all events of a

cultural nature that could raise the 'prestige' of the fascists among the people. S a b o t a g e in all branches of the fine arts which are in the least con-nected with and serve National Socialism.
S a b o t a g e in all literature, all newspapers, which stand in the pay of the 'government', fight for its ideas, for the spreading of the brown lie. Do not sacrifice a penny in street collections (even if they are carried out under the guise of charitable pur-poses). Because this is only a camouflage.
In reality, the result does not benefit the Red Cross or the needy. The government does not need this money, is not financially dependent on these collections—the printing presses run continuously and produce any amount of paper money. The people, however, must be kept constantly in suspense, the pressure of the curb must never slacken! Give nothing to the metal, textile and other collections. Seek to convince all acquaintances, even from the lower class of the popu-lation, of the futility of a continuation, of the hope-lessness of this war, of the spiritual and economic enslavement, of the destruction of all moral and reli-gious values by National Socialism, and to induce them to p a s s i v e r e s i s t a n c e !

-- -- -- -- -- -- -- -- --

Aristotle, 'On Politics': '..... Furthermore it be-longs (to the essence of tyranny) to strive that noth-ing remains hidden what any subject speaks or does, but everywhere spies eavesdrop on him, ... to incite all the world against each other and to enmity friends with friends and the people with the nobles and the rich among themselves. Then it belongs to such tyrannical measures to make the subjects poor, so that the bodyguard can be paid, and they, occupied with the care of their daily acquisition, have no time and leisure to instigate conspiracies..... Furthermore, such high income taxes as those imposed in Syracuse, for under Dionysius the citizens of that state had happily spent all their wealth in taxes in five years. And also constantly to excite wars, the tyrant is inclined...'

Please duplicate and share!!!

FOURTH LEAFLET OF THE WHITE ROSE (1942)

Leaflets of the White Rose

IV

It is an old wisdom that is preached to children over and over again, that he who will not listen must feel. But a clever child will burn his fingers only once on the hot stove.

In the past weeks Hitler had successes in Africa as well as in Russia. The result was that optimism on the one side, dismay and pessimism on the other side of the people rose with a rapidity incomparable to German inertia. Everywhere among Hitler's opponents, that is, among the better part of the people, one heard cries of lamentation, words of disappointment and discouragement, which not infrequently ended in the exclamation: 'Should Hitler now...?'

Meanwhile, the German attack on Egypt has come to a halt, Rommel must remain in a dangerously exposed position, but still the advance in the east continues. This apparent success has been bought at the most horrible sacrifices, so that it can no longer be called advantageous. We therefore warn against a n y optimism.

Who counted the dead, Hitler or Goebbels—probably neither of them. Thousands are falling every day in Russia. It is the time of harvest, and the reaper drives full speed into the ripe seed. Mourning returns to the huts of the homeland and no one is there to dry the tears of the mothers, but Hitler lies to those whose dearest possessions he has robbed and driven to senseless death.

Every word that comes out of Hitler's mouth is a lie. When he says peace, he means war, and when he calls the name of the Almighty in the most sacrilegious manner, he means the power of evil, the fallen angel, Satan. His mouth is the stinking maw of hell, and his power is basically rejected. It is true that the struggle against the National Socialist terrorist state must be waged by rational means; but anyone who still doubts the real existence of the demonic powers today has by no means grasped the metaphysical background of this war. Behind the concrete, behind the sensually perceptible, behind all factual, logical considerations, there is the irrational, i.e. the fight against the demon, against the messenger of the Antichrist.

Everywhere and at all times the demons have lurked in the darkness for the hour when man becomes weak, when he arbitrarily leaves his position in the ordo [order], which was given to him by God on the basis of freedom, when he gives in to the pressure of evil, breaks away from the powers of a higher order and thus, after he has voluntarily taken the first step, everywhere and at all times of greatest need men have risen up, prophets, saints, who had preserved their freedom, who pointed to the One and Only God and with His help exhorted the people to repentance. Man is free, but he is defenceless against evil without the true God, he is like a ship without a rudder, abandoned to the storm, like an infant without a mother, like a cloud that dissolves.

Is there, I ask you, who are a Christian, in this struggle for the preservation of your highest goods, a hesitation, a game of intrigue, a postponement of the decision in the hope that another will take up arms to defend you? Has not God Himself given you the strength and courage to fight? We m u s t attack evil where it is most powerful, and it is most powerful in the power of Hitler.

'Again I saw all the oppressions that are practiced under the sun. And behold, the tears of the oppressed, and they had no one to comfort them! On the side of their oppressors there was power, and there was no one to comfort them.

And I thought the dead who are already dead more fortunate than the living who are still alive...'

(Proverbs)

[The correct source is Ecclesiastes 4: 1–2.]

Novalis: 'True anarchy is the begetting element of religion. Out of the destruction of everything positive it raises its glorious head as the new founder of the world.... If Europe wanted to awaken again, if a state of states, a political science were imminent! Should the hierarchy... be the principle of the union of states?... Blood will flow over Europe until the nations become aware of their terrible madness, which drives them around in circles, and, struck and soothed by sacred music, step to former altars in colourful mingling, perform works of peace and celebrate a great peace festival on the smoking battlefields with hot tears. Only religion can reawaken Europe and secure the law of nations and install Christendom with new glory visibly on earth in its peacemaking office.'

We expressly point out that the White Rose does not stand in the pay of a foreign power. Although we know that the National Socialist power must be broken militarily, we seek a renewal of the severely wounded German spirit from within. This rebirth, however, must be preceded by a clear realization of all the guilt which the German people have incurred and by a ruthless struggle against Hitler and his all too many accomplices, party members, quislings, and so on. With all brutality the gulf between the better part of the people and everything connected with National Socialism must be torn open. For Hitler and his followers there is no punishment on this earth that would be just to their deeds.

But out of love for future generations, an example must be made after the end of the war, so that no one should ever feel the slightest desire to try something similar again. Do not forget also the small scoundrels of this system, remember the names, so that none escapes! They shall not succeed in changing the flag at the last minute after these atrocities and pretend that nothing has happened!

For your reassurance we would like to add that the addresses of the readers of the White Rose are nowhere written down. The addresses are taken arbitrarily from address books.

We will not keep silent, we are your guilty conscience; the White Rose will not leave you in peace!

Please duplicate and send on!

THE FIFTH WHITE ROSE LEAFLET (1943)

Leaflets of The Resistance Movement in Germany.

Call to all Germans!

The war is approaching its certain end. As in 1918, the German government is trying to draw all attention to the growing submarine danger, while in the East the armies are pouring back ceaselessly, in the West the invasion is expected. America's armament has not yet reached its peak, but today it already surpasses anything in history since. With mathematical certainty Hitler leads the German people into the abyss. Hitler cannot win the war, only prolong it! His and his helpers' guilt has infinitely exceeded every measure. The just punishment is coming closer and closer!

But what do the German people do? It does not see and it does not hear. Blindly it follows its seducers into ruin. Victory at any price! they have written on their banner. I will fight to the last man, says Hitler —but the war is already lost.

Germans! Do you and your children want to suffer the same fate that befell the Jews? Do you want to be measured by the same yardstick as your seducers? Shall we forever be the people hated and rejected by the whole world? No! Therefore, separate yourselves from the National Socialist subhumanity [Untermenschentum]! Prove by deed that you think differently! A new war of liberation is dawning. The better part of the people fights on our side. Tear the cloak of indifference that you have wrapped around your heart! Decide b e f o r e it is too late!

Do not believe the National Socialist propaganda which has put the Bolshevik fright into your limbs! Do not believe that Germany's salvation is bound up for better or worse with the victory of National Socialism! Criminalism cannot win a German victory. Separate yourselves i n t i m e from everything connected with National Socialism! Afterwards, a terrible but just judgment will come upon those who cowardly and indecisively kept themselves hidden.

What does the outcome of this war, which was never a national one, teach us?

The imperialist idea of power, from whatever side it may come, must be rendered harmless for all time. A one-sided Prussian militarism must never again come to power. Only in generous cooperation of the European peoples can the ground be created on which a new construction will be possible. Every centralistic power, such as the Prussian state has tried to exercise in Germany and Europe, must be nipped in the bud. The coming Germany can only be federalist. Only a healthy federalist order of states can today fill the weakened Europe with new life. The working class must be freed from its state of lowest slavery by a sensible socialism. The illusion of a self-sufficient economy must disappear in Europe. Every people, every individual has a right to the goods of the world!

Freedom of speech, freedom of confession, protection of the individual citizen against the arbitrariness of criminal violent states, these are the foundations of the new Europe.

Support the resistance movement, spread the leaflets!

THE SIXTH LEAFLET OF THE WHITE ROSE (1943)

Fellow [female] students! Fellow [male] students!

Shocked, our nation stands before the downfall of the men of Stalingrad. Three hundred and thirty thousand German men have been senselessly and irresponsibly hounded to their death and destruction by the ingenious strategy of the World War corporal. Führer, we thank you!

There is a ferment in the German people: Do we want to continue to entrust the fate of our armies to a dilettante? Do we want to sacrifice the rest of our German youth to the lowest power instincts of a party clique? Nevermore!

The day of reckoning has come, the reckoning of the German youth with the most despicable tyranny our people has ever endured. In the name of all German youth we demand from the state of Adolf Hitler the return of personal freedom, the most precious good of the Germans, of which he has cheated us in the most pitiful way.

We grew up in a state of ruthless gagging of every free expression of opinion. HJ, SA and SS tried to uniformize, revolutionize and narcotise us during the most fruitful educational years of our lives. 'Weltanschauliche Schulung' (ideological training) was the contemptible method of smothering sprouting self-thinking and self-esteem in a fog of empty phrases. A selection of leaders, as it cannot be thought more diabolical and at the same time more narrow-minded, raises its future party bigwigs on order castles to godless, shameless and conscience-

less exploiters and murder boys, to the blind, dumb-
founded following of leaders. We 'Intellectual Work-
ers' are the ones who should put obstacles in the way
of this new ruling class. Front-line fighters are
reprimanded by student leaders and Gauleiter aspir-
ants like schoolboys, Gauleiters attack the honour of
female students with lecherous jokes. <u>German female
students at the Munich University have given a dig-
nified answer to the sullying of their honour,</u> German
students have stood up for their female comrades and
stood firm. This is a beginning of the fight for our
free self-determination, without which spiritual
values cannot be created. Our thanks go to the brave
comrades who led by shining example!

There is only one slogan for us: War against the
party! Leave the party branches where they want to
keep us politically muzzled! Get out of the lecture
halls of the SS Unterführer or Oberführer and party
bootlickers! We are concerned with true science and
genuine freedom of thought! No threat can frighten us,
not even the closure of our universities. It is the
struggle of each one of us for our future, our freedom
and honour in a state conscious of its moral responsibility.

Freedom and honour! For ten long years, Hitler and
his comrades have squeezed these two glorious German
words ad nauseam, trashed them, twisted them, as only
dilettantes are able to do, throwing the highest values of a nation before the swine. What freedom and
honour mean to them, they have shown sufficiently in
ten years of destruction of all material and spiritual
freedom, of all moral substance in the German people.
Even the dumbest German has opened his eyes to the
terrible bloodbath which they have wrought through-

out Europe in the name of freedom and honour of the German nation and are wreaking anew every day. The German name will remain desecrated forever unless the German youth finally stands up, avenges and atones at the same time, smashes their tormentors and erects a new spiritual Europe.

[Female] <u>Students!</u> [Male] <u>Students! The German people is looking to us!</u> From us it expects, <u>as in 1813 the</u> breaking of the Napoleonic, so in 1943 the breaking of the National Socialist terror from the power of the spirit. Beresina and Stalingrad flare up in the East, the dead of Stalingrad summon us!

'Wake up my people, the flame signs are smoking!' Our people are standing in the awakening against the enslavement of Europe by National Socialism, in the new believing breakthrough before freedom and honour!

15

Appendix: Resources

➤ Join the resistance and receive our newsletter: *thewhiterose.uk/newsletter*
➤ Here you can find leaflets for downloading and further resources: *thewhiterose.uk/downloads*
➤ Book recommendations: *thewhiterose.uk/books*
➤ Another book published by The White Rose UK: *Freedom! An Anthology of Poems, Short Stories and Essays. Composed by 36 Authors Questioning Covid Restrictions and Lockdowns* (March 2021)
➤ For more research, type in keywords in the search field on *thewhiterose.uk*. There are currently over 800 articles on the website.
➤ Film about the German resistance group: *The White Rose*, 1983, by Michael Verhoeven, starring Lena Stolze and Wulf Kessler
➤ Look up reported deaths and adverse reactions to the covid injection (only about 1–10% of the actual number of adverse reactions and deaths are reported): Yellow Card on *UK Column News.*

Special thanks to all proofreaders, the many subscribers and everyone else supporting our resistance!

Printed in Great Britain
by Amazon